Magnificat

Magnificat

The Journey and the Song

ELIZABETH RUTH OBBARD

Paulist Press
New York/Mahwah

First published in Great Britain by Darton, Longman & Todd Ltd

Library of Congress Cataloging-in-Publication Data

Obbard, Elizabeth Ruth, 1945–
    Magnificat : the journey and the song.

    1. Magnificat—Meditations.   2. Spiritual life—
Catholic authors.   I. Title.
BS2595.4.032   1986   242'.722   86-9454
ISBN 0-8091-2833-0 (pbk.)

Published by Paulist Press
997 Macarthur Boulevard
Mahwah, N.J. 07430

Printed and bound in the United States of America

For Rachel
with love and gratitude

Contents

Acknowledgements   viii

Introduction   ix

Visitation   1

Loved by the Lord   8

Established in Peace   15

Growing in Love   23

Self and God   29

Wounded for Glory   35

A Heart of Compassion   43

The Blossoming Desert   51

Fruitful in Surrender   57

All is His Gift   63

Witnesses to Grace   68

Bearing His Likeness   75

A New Song   81

Acknowledgements

All substantial scriptural quotations are taken from *The Jerusalem Bible*, published and copyright 1966, 1967 and 1968 by Darton, Longman and Todd Ltd and Doubleday & Co Inc, by permission of the publishers.

I am grateful to Jean Vials for allowing me to quote her poem, 'The Jewish Bride'.

ELIZABETH RUTH OBBARD
Carmel of Our Lady of Walsingham
Norfolk

Introduction

From the long window of my room at Langham Carmel I look out over the gently rolling fields of Norfolk towards Walsingham, 'England's Nazareth', four miles away. The presence of Mary seems very near — as if I myself would at any moment glimpse her coming over those low hills, bearing within her the Child she has conceived.

The wide skies, filled with wheeling seagulls, are for me a symbol of that freedom to which we all aspire. Norfolk is somehow a land which facilitates inner space, with its clear vistas and flat fields opening onto limitless horizons.

Here Julian of Norwich, England's greatest mystic, grew from girlhood to womanhood, her spirit entwined with that of the child Mary of her *Revelations*. And in the same way each one of us grows from youth to maturity, from seedling to sunflower, from solitude to community.

For me, the mystery of the Visitation in Luke's Gospel is the mystery of this growth — from God being a gift to me alone, to his being a gift to others through me. How truly I've experienced this in my life! He has led me by the self-giving of others through whom he shone as a home-light to my searching young heart. He has led me by way of an old Cenacle nun who took me under her wing as 'my child Elizabeth' and then on into the enduring friendships of my maturer years.

He has taken me from my first faltering steps in religious life when as a self-centred and rebellious teen-ager I approached the altar to receive the habit, asking that there might re-echo in my heart the words blazoned above it — *Ecce Ancilla Domini*, 'behold the handmaid of the Lord' — to the desert peace of my Solemn Profession as a Carmelite after a long, lonely journey — a journey which still continues into an unknown future.

Life is always a moving on, a hearing of the word of God where we are, a rising up to communicate with others, to share for a moment. Then listening anew, rising anew, enriched by contact, friendship and human warmth. Each phase of life contains its own dying, to rise like the phoenix from the familiar ashes of the home hearth.

Therefore I offer this book from my heart to all those who have been for me carriers of the Lord, as I hope and pray I have been for others in my turn; to those who have opened my eyes to what it means to be God's woman, and have encouraged me to keep journeying towards my goal. And I ask the Lord to make of each of our lives an echo of Mary's own Magnificat:

My soul proclaims the greatness of the Lord
and my spirit exults in God my saviour.

Mary set out at that time and went as quickly as she could to a town in the hill country of Judah. She went into Zechariah's house and greeted Elizabeth. Now as soon as Elizabeth heard Mary's greeting, the child leapt in her womb and Elizabeth was filled with the Holy Spirit. She gave a loud cry and said, 'Of all women you are the most blessed, and blessed is the fruit of your womb. Why should I be honoured with a visit from the mother of my Lord? For the moment your greeting reached my ears, the child in my womb leapt for joy. Yes, blessed is she who believed that the promise made her by the Lord would be fulfilled.' And Mary said:

'My soul proclaims the greatness of the Lord
and my spirit exults in God my saviour;
because he has looked upon his lowly handmaid.
Yes, from this day forward all generations will call me
*   blessed,*
for the Almighty has done great things for me.
Holy is his name,
and his mercy reaches from age to age for those who
*   fear him.*
He has shown the power of his arm,
he has routed the proud of heart.
He has pulled down princes from their thrones and
*   exalted the lowly.*
The hungry he has filled with good things, the rich sent
*   empty away.*
He has come to the help of Israel his servant, mindful
*   of his mercy*
—according to the promise he made to our ancestors—
of his mercy to Abraham and to his descendants
*   forever.'*

Mary stayed with Elizabeth about three months and then went back home.

(Luke 1: 39–56)

Visitation

The mystery of the encounter between Mary and Elizabeth finds an echo in the lives of all women. Mary and Elizabeth are linked inseparably as are Ruth and Naomi, mother and daughter, young and old. Mary is the archetypal woman who bears the Lord within her and awakens another to a living response.

Mary, like Ruth, travels from what are the dear and familiar surroundings of home to the hill country of Judah; and yet there she too is affirmed in a new way, no longer an alien but a life-bearer, life-sharer. The seed of the Word, nourished in her womb, makes Mary a Christ-carrier in the fullest sense.

If there is any scriptural story that speaks to my heart and sheds light on what it means to be a woman, not merely today, but down through the ages, it is this one. The journey of Mary's life finds expression in a song, a service, and then silence, as she ponders these things in her heart. So must we ponder upon life, upon the Word, upon God's presence in the midst of life's ordinary happenings.

After the angel's greeting and announcement of the coming birth of the Messiah Mary arose and went 'as quickly as she could' to the hill country of Judah. Like

1

the bride of the Song of Songs the new life of spring is about her and within her. God is calling:

> Come then, my love,
> my lovely one, come.
> For see, winter is past,
> the rains are over and gone.
> The flowers appear on the earth.
> The season of glad songs has come . . .
> The fig tree is forming its first figs
> and the blossoming vines give out their fragrance.
>
> (S. of S. 2:10–13)

Mary goes, not consciously to bring Christ to another. She merely reaches out to another in need, the power of human devotion overcomes any natural shrinking.

Della Robbia's sculpture of the Visitation sums up everything so beautifully. In it one sees the grave, tender face of Mary, conscious of the Child growing beneath her heart. Elizabeth kneels, reaching towards her, intent, searching. Each woman is more concerned for the other than for self. Mary for Elizabeth, who is to bear a child in old age to gladden her previous barrenness; Elizabeth for Mary, who is mother of the Messiah, as yet so young, so inexperienced in life's trials. Linked together in stone they summarise the generations of women from time immemorial — their mutual support and understanding mirror an interior reality that lies hidden beneath the day-to-day exterior events of life, in which the presence of God can be discerned by sensitive persons, aware of another dimension. It is as if Mary is saying to Elizabeth: 'Don't kneel to me. We are equals, you and I; each loved and chosen by the Lord

in our own way. Virginity and motherhood are indissolubly intertwined in us. We are the bearers of salvation's promise, what is fine and beautiful has been entrusted to our care. What more could we desire when God is our All, and in him we know fulfilment.'

The song that Luke places on the lips of Mary at this juncture of her life is the Magnificat. Biblical scholars think this could well have been originally a hymn of the anawim, Israel's lowly, trustful followers of Yahweh, which was later attributed to the mother of God. Be that as it may, surely it expresses the very heart of

3

her spirituality, a spirituality with which each of us can identify.

Here is a song of joy rising from a background of shame and suffering. Mary is in the position of an unmarried mother, she does not know what the future holds for her, and yet in this situation there bursts forth a paean of praise as Elizabeth greets her, 'blessed is she who believed'.

Yes, Mary believed when all was going wrong, when her life wasn't taking the course she had originally chosen for herself. In going to help and comfort her cousin was she not hoping to receive help and comfort in return? And God speaks through Elizabeth's lips. Mary has believed and trusted despite everything. All is well. The promise is being completed in her life in ways she cannot understand intellectually, but can grasp at the deepest non-conceptual level. She is the Lord's handmaid. He will not desert her.

Like Ruth, Mary is rewarded a hundredfold.

Like Ruth she has chosen Yahweh for her lot with no guarantees.

She comes to another place prepared to accept hardships and to labour out of love. That is enough.

Mary's love and service given to Elizabeth is blessed as was Ruth's to Naomi, by combined joy over a child of promise. The Holy Spirit is activated and Mary realises her unique role in salvation history. Yes, God has done *everything* for her and in her. The poverty of her virginity, of her empty waiting, has borne fruit a hundredfold. Jesus came to his own and his own received him not; but here is a glimpse of two women who *did* receive him and were humble enough to recognise his hidden presence.

In some way, the Visitation is the mystery of Christ growing in each one of us. The seed of the Word is meant to germinate in the waters of our baptism. We are to be Christ-bearers for the world, sharing him in our ordinary human exchanges. Even if he is only a tiny embryo we can awaken new, responsive life in others. What a strange power there is in one who bears the Lord! She is never alone, and as she matures the Life within makes her more keenly sensitive to the inner life of those about her. But all this in a most natural way, for the supernatural has become incarnate in her own flesh. She shines with the radiance of one who bears the Light of the World.

Mary stands at the apex of a long line of praying men and women who have longed for the Messiah. In her being she symbolises the yearning of Israel, the yearning of all of us, to be redeemed. Purified, she is able to repose trustfully upon her God. Limpid to reflect him, she has the candour of one who has known no kind of defilement. Her refuge is in the Lord — how can she be afraid when she is so surely protected?

> In your midst I will leave
> a humble and lowly people,
> and those who are left in Israel
> will seek refuge in the name of Yahweh.
> They will do no wrong,
> will tell no lies . . .
> But they will be able to graze and rest
> with no one to disturb them. (Zeph. 3:12–13)

Mary was one of these lowly ones and so God was able to be her shepherd in a pre-eminent manner. She was one who never deviated from her vocation because she listened continually to the calling forth of God within her. She is the woman wholly given to him, for others. What she has accepted in herself is to be extended to all. The one who says 'yes' cannot halt there, for a woman longs to give life, to diffuse life, to bear life, for love of another. To be fruitful her love must extend beyond herself or it withers within her. The desert must blossom or there is only dry dust.

And thus Mary is grateful — grateful for everything. For the bewilderment, for the joy, for the pain, for God's choice of and use of her. God is within her, how can she be afraid? She can in her Magnificat anticipate the outburst of John of the Cross as it dawns upon him that he already has everything; nothing can be wanting to the one who possesses the Lord:

> O thou soul, most beautiful of creatures, who so longest to know the place where thy Beloved is that thou mayest seek him and be united to him. Thou knowest now that thou art thyself that very tabernacle where he dwells, the secret chamber of his retreat where he is hidden. Rejoice therefore and exult, because all thy good and all thy hope is so near thee as to be within thee; or, to speak more accurately, that thou cans't not be without it, 'for lo the kingdom of God is within you'.
>
> (*Spiritual Canticle* st. i)

This knowledge of God as our ever present companion is the joy of the saints, for barren loneliness is the greatest destroyer of the human heart, whereas loving intimacy brings it to flower.

Mary is the one who can share with us the secret of her own joy. The Lord is with her always. She knows in reality what we know by faith. And so she comes up from the wilderness of Judah 'leaning upon her beloved' (S. of S. 8:5).

Loved by the Lord

Perhaps one way into the mystery of Mary is to see her in the context of other biblical women. 'To win Rachel Jacob worked seven years, and they seemed to him but a few days because of the greatness of his love' (Gen. 29:20). Woman is the beloved, 'chosen' and important. She it is who calls forth the best in man. Isaac and Jacob, we are told, both *loved* their wives.

As the homemaker a Jewish woman had great influence on her children. She was the joy of her husband, the beacon light of the house, and we see her presiding there with the benevolence of a sacred person.

> Like the sun rising over the mountains of the Lord
> is the beauty of a good wife in a well-kept house.
> Like the lamp shining on the sacred lampstand
> is a beautiful face on a well-proportioned body.
> (Ecclus. 26:21–2)

In woman the beauty of God is made present. She possesses the gift of radiance.

What endows a woman with radiance is the conviction that she is loved, and by being loved she becomes ever more lovable. We must then exercise our faith in God's love for us, even when we feel nothing. We have been set up to shine in his Church, and so must reflect in our flesh the knowledge that we are cherished.

To be radiant is to be a woman responsive to God and to others. It is a contradiction to bear the light yoke of the Lord as if it were a heavy burden. Do we not desire to respond gladly to God's love? And if there is no free response then there is no love for ultimately love can only be freely given. The women of the patriarchal period of the Old Testament glow with radiant human personalities — they are free with the desert freedom of the nomad. Rachel and Leah live for us today, as do Sarah and Rebecca; they laugh, rejoice, exhibit jealousy, favouritism, independence, reciprocal love. They are no mere appendages to their husbands! They are the forerunners of the women we meet in the New Testament — Mary of Nazareth, Anna, Mary Magdalen, Mary of Bethany, Martha, Dorcas, the persistent Syro-Phoenician, the widow of Nain.

Woman mirrors two aspects of life, activity and contemplation, united in one soul. When perfectly harmonised on both these scores she is an image of God himself, in whom masculine and feminine are synthesised and transcended.

Perhaps we can see this most clearly in the figures of Rachel and Leah that Michelangelo has placed either side of his masterly statue of Moses the lawgiver. They are the Old Testament equivalent of Martha and Mary depicted either side of Jesus. They are symbols of the two facets of woman. In his sculpture Michelangelo uses Rachel as the figure of faith, the contemplative life. She is the loved one for whom Jacob laboured, she has that inner confidence of the chosen woman, and so she looks upward with great trust. Her dress falls carelessly

about her, and she wears the veil of the married woman, beloved of her lord. She has but one foot on the ground so that she inclines towards heaven rather than towards earth. Rachel persevered in her faith even though she knew many years of barrenness, and her fidelity was rewarded by the birth of two sons. God has made the barren to dwell in the home, the joyful mother of children.

Leah, on the other hand, is symbolic of the life of active love. In her humility she looks downwards. She knew she was not particularly dear to Jacob but she herself loved and gave all she had with utter selflessness. Her hair is therefore braided and coiled up for work; she labours without looking for reward. Her feet are both placed firmly on the ground; her dress is tucked up ready for household tasks, but beautiful in contrast to Rachel's gown — she wants to look pleasing. In her right hand she carries spun wool, for she is always at work under the eye of God (symbolised in the motif of her wool band, upon which is chiselled the all-seeing cherubim). In her left hand she bears the bridal wreath. The joy and happiness of her wedding lasted but a day, to be followed by years of labour and sorrow. She lacks Rachel's glowing self-confidence.

Leah did not experience love's ecstasy, yet she faithfully bore Jacob children and did not return to her father's house. There was in her no sign of jealousy. She is *herself* just as Rachel is herself. And strangely it is through Leah, not Rachel, that the Messiah is to come, for Leah is the mother of Judah.

These two women are in all of us. We have a contemplative side and an active side. We are Rachel and Leah, Martha and Mary: at one moment surrendering to love, at another labouring to give when we feel nothing. Our contemplative side is full of faith and confidence. It knows God's choice, looks continually to him. This is our veiled side, the mysterious self-gift hidden even from ourselves. Body and soul belong to God — how we know not; we can but keep our eyes fixed on him and allow him to enfold us with the bridal veil. Our active side at its best labours without looking for reward; it is humble and self-distrustful, desiring only to give to the beloved. It takes nothing for granted.

Action and contemplation are summed up in Mary, the perfect woman. She is wholly receptive, yet wholly self-giving. She receives to give.

Mary is pure receptivity, ground ready to receive the seed. She is the garden of the Lord, image of beauty and holiness. And as receptive ground she blossoms with a rich variety of flowers and plants.

Mountains and hills will break into joyful cries before you

and all the trees of the countryside clap their hands.
Cypress will grow instead of thorns,
myrtle instead of briars.
And this will make Yahweh famous,
a sign for ever, ineffaceable. (Isa. 55:12–13)

The receptive barren land becomes, by accepting the
Word of God, fruitful beyond compare. Our Lady is
the most beautiful of women because in the soil of her
heart and of her body God himself was brought forth
for the world. In her the Word was made flesh.

In the liturgy Mary is linked with Israel, personified
as the daughter of Sion. She springs from the Jewish
people, bears the seeds of the Old Testament and the
flowers of the New. 'Sion shall be called mother for all
shall be her children' (Ps. 48). She is the woman tied to
God's land, linked physically, spiritually, psychologi-
cally, with her own people. The wholeness of her personality is the root of Christ's who unites Jew and
Gentile. He unites *because* he was so consciously a Jew,
secure in the love of the One God — his Father.
Through Mary we are brought to God's holy mountain,
Jesus, and made joyful in his house of prayer — for it
is a house of prayer for *all* peoples — no one is excluded
(Isa. 56:7).

In the Gospels Mary symbolises the true disciple, the
'poor one' who clings to the Lord. She is shown
pondering God's word, responding to it at the Annunciation, taking him to others in the Visitation, bringing
him forth at the Nativity, accepting his sorrowful
destiny at the Presentation and by the foot of the Cross.
She is a woman who enters deeply into every aspect of
her Son. She is not merely the mother of Christ, but

mother of the mystical Christ, the Church, whose perfect image she is as bride of the Lamb.

Woman in herself is the basic symbol of the surrendered soul. She is timeless, at the root of all life, bound by the rhythms of nature to the cycle of regeneration. In her receptivity woman is bride and mother, available for the experience of God's deepest love and for burgeoning with new life. Mary is supremely the surrendered one whose virginity was overshadowed by the Holy Spirit, making her fruitful in motherhood. She is the soul in its relationship to God.

John of the Cross and Teresa of Avila loved to compare the soul to a garden, receptive to wind, water and seed, a 'garden enclosed' for the divine Lover.

But like Mary, our soul is a garden not for self but to give joy to Another. Like her, our passive, 'Rachel' role is actually playing an active part in the redemption. Nothing is received solely for ourselves, but for him, and through him for others. Mary's 'Leah' role, her activity, consisted in responding to all that was asked of her — all the tasks of Jewish motherhood which, though so mundane, held deep religious significance. Surely her overflowing love and care for her family, her cooking, her cleaning, her contacts with friends and neighbours would draw from her the surprised cry at the end of her life 'Lord, *when* did we see you cold, hungry, naked . . . and cared for you?'

Mary knew the heartbreak of seeing her Son move away from her to his own independent life, and then saw that same life snuffed out so cruelly in a death where the Innocent One was tortured by the powerful. Through it all she is trusting, silently pondering, always receding into the background.

13

Woman is called to be the hidden feminine principle in an overly masculine Church, fostering Christ's life in herself and in others. She is Marian in the deepest, completest sense of the word.

Mary is the companion of the soul's solitude since she too has known human isolation.

Mary is the model of continual prayer as she ponders the Word of God and receives the Spirit.

Mary is the woman who embraced *life* with all its sufferings and hardships. Yet she did this with joy, looking not at herself but only at the larger world held in the orbit of the Father's love.

Mary is the one who pleased God always — by her initial 'fiat' sustained by a life of surrender. In her is exemplified the saying of her Son: 'Not everyone who calls me Lord, Lord, shall enter the kingdom, but she who does the will of my Father in heaven.'

Established in Peace[1]

When Mary set out to visit Elizabeth she set out from her own home. What a message there is here for our rootless, restless society. We *need* to be rooted, to be identified with a place we can call 'home' — where we are at ease, accepted in good days and bad, to which we can always return and be sure of a welcome. The plant without roots withers away.

We cannot set out on a journey unless we first have a place to leave. If we know not where we come from how shall we discover a way to another goal? Each man under his own vine and fig tree, seated at his own table with wife and children, are scriptural images of perception. We have need of initial security.

In our memory, the recollection of places is unique. If you close your eyes and move gently back to your childhood what do you see? ... the familiar living-room with the torn sofa in a corner; the bedroom with its acquired 'treasures', stone collections, books; the patch of garden where you played at being 'little grey rabbit', with your brother and sister as hare and squirrel; the line of blueberry bushes which you picked

---

[1] I am indebted to Paul Tournier's book *A Place for You* for some of the ideas expressed in this chapter.

so freely and then were found out because of your purple-stained teeth. . . . These vignettes are clearer than any particular face, however much loved, more enduring than any words. Our early environment continues to affect us all through life. The person who is 'at home' in the place of his childhood is 'at home' anywhere.

God, as the God of history, has revealed himself in particular places at particular times. He intervenes in Mary's life while she is at Nazareth, but he is not bound to Nazareth alone. He can only be kept and held in being given. And so Mary rises to meet Elizabeth at Ain Karim. She is 'on pilgrimage' with her Lord.

Are there not places too where we knew God to be close to us, where grace has had a special impact on our hearts, where we can return again in memory to taste anew the sweetness of his presence? The church crib at Christmas with its magical lights where it was first borne in upon our tender souls that God had come to earth as a Child asking for our love; the spot by a tumbling waterfall where we were struck by a moment of decision and saw clearly what path the Lord had planned for our life, and knew that we must set off resolutely along our appointed way. . . . And yet, the Lord does not remain in the past but is with us now on life's pilgrimage. We belong to all the scenes we have passed through and are still moving on to others.

One way to a more profound understanding of the inner life of someone else is to understand them as it were 'in their place'. We know Mary better by learning of a Jewish woman's life of the same period in Palestine; we see Teresa of Avila under the burning sun of medieval Spain with its savage natural and religious

16

extremes; Thérèse of Lisieux in the plush comfort of the nineteenth-century French bourgeoisie; Elizabeth of Hungary amid the splendours of a court of minne-singers, yet viewing extreme misery and poverty outside the castle walls.

Jesus too was a man of his own particular place. From being firmly grounded in his own family with its accepting love, its particular Davidic heritage, its religious and social customs, he was able to develop as he matured in a way that was uniquely his own. Through human trust in his parents he was enabled to discover the utter trustworthiness of the Father and be at home in his presence. His early life must have been unspeakably wonderful to have produced this flower of perfect manhood. Having had a place in childhood he was later able to mix freely with all men even while, materially speaking, he had no place to lay his head. His disciples he says are to make their home in him, completely secure in his care.

But before we can offer hospitality to another we have to be at home in ourselves. We cannot renounce security unless we have it to renounce. We must learn human trust in order to experience the divine. We cannot receive the hundredfold promised to those who leave all for Christ unless we have attached ourselves to things at the proper time. Nazareth is the image of a security that was necessary as a preparation for Calvary.

In the early days of Christianity the family was taken for granted as the basic social unit, as it was in Judaism. It wasn't considered necessary for preachers to comment on the obvious; they were concerned with developing dogma, coming to terms with philosophical thought.

Then came the fragmentation of the Church, the break up of Christendom, the founding of independent nations, a new commercial mobility. As society changed so the nuclear family assumed new importance, and the Holy Family took on religious significance for the ordinary Christian. In a changing world how would children find security if not in the home?

So we see those wonderful paintings of Dutch interiors with their ordered homeliness! The shining tiles of Pieter de Hooch and the clean austere studios of Vermeer, filled with light. There is Vermeer's quaint 'little street' redolent of childhood memories, and his panoramic picture of Delft, his beloved city, a visible image of the heavenly Jerusalem, 'blest city of peace'. Heaven lies about Vermeer in his home and his city. There is Rembrandt's 'Holy Family' in the Hermitage Gallery, with our Lady a typically plump young Dutch housewife bending solicitously over the cradle where her baby keeps warm beneath a snug red blanket, while in the shadows Joseph plies his carpenter's trade. Through the dimness a diagonal of small cherubs play above the child, shining angels' wings illumine the earth, concealing God's glory in domestic ordinariness. The Holy Family is every family in its familiar setting.

Every person needs a place to 'be', for our concept of who we are is bound up to where we belong. A woman above all needs to discover her life's vocation and root herself there in the soil of everyday life, be it marriage and family, career, profession or the consecrated religious calling. Flights of the spirit come to nothing, dreams remain but dreams, unless they are nourished in the firm earth of daily life. To find one's vocation is to find where one is 'at home', and it is to be there not only exteriorly but interiorly also — for if one withdraws interior 'presence' from a place, one is driven to move elsewhere even physically.

And so, we must each be rooted deeply in the soil of our family, our community, our work, our particular surroundings. We need to belong fully where we live, and this involves respect and understanding for those who share our lives. We need to develop a contemplative attitude towards things, as did the Dutch housewife of old with her shining sideboard, her polished windowbox. Once we have learnt to live in the ordinary, then, and only then, can we begin to move into the deeper, as yet undreamed-of vistas that open within us.

St Benedict has a telling sentence in his Rule when he says that the most mundane household implements of the monastery should be treated with the same reverence as the vessels of the altar. We today consciously try to plan beautiful liturgies in our Churches, but what of the liturgy of daily life which is our special sphere? We should bring everything to this priestly task of ours. Of what use are ecological campaigns when our senses are totally out of tune with the plain beauty of home? We need to remind ourselves that we make our environment and then our environment makes us — where and how we live changes us as persons. We casually fill our houses with expensive gadgets, fancy bric-a-brac or the tubular steel hardness of terminals and cafés. Everyone needs rather to be surrounded by cherished, well-made things, and these need not be expensive. I can see in my mind's eye my grandmother's semi-detached house near Wakefield — its cleanliness, the lovingly embroidered cloths, the scrubbed step, the currant pastry laid out

ready for buttering. These are simple things, but they impress a child with a sense of order and rightness. This is why housing needs to be high on our priority list. A home where people can live with dignity is not an extra but an essential. It is a 'thou' place which creates and recreates the ones who live there. The traditional monastic environment of clean austerity is as much part of religion as church services. The liturgy of an ordered life establishes hearts in peace, just as carelessness, dirt, haste do damage to people and surroundings. Competence and care are not opposing but complementary companions. As we rediscover our home area through a more contemplative attitude to the stuff of the world, so we grow in appreciation of others as they are, and not just as we would like them to be

Jesus offers new life, but we cannot accept it unless we are first practised in living. All spiritual and psychological writers agree that we cannot move into new levels without a thorough assimilation of earlier stages of growth. Before we can make discoveries, or become experts, we must first be rooted in traditional and basic skills.

Before universalising we must particularise. God must be *my* God before I can give him to others, and this Mary demonstrates for us. She receives the Word in the security of home, yet she forthwith rises to respond to another's need. By her proper attachment she is able to detach herself when the time is ripe.

God wants to lead us beyond security too, to give us new birth, new life. But the way there must pass first through the liturgy of our ordinary occupations. Nazareth is basic spirituality, and without a base how can anything stand on immovable foundations?

Growing in Love

 To leave ourselves to go on love's journey, the journey to God, involves detachment. It means being ready to set out when he asks us. It means cleaving to him with such trust that we are enabled ultimately to make our home in him alone.

In search of my Love
I will go over mountains and strands;
I will gather no flowers,
I will fear no wild beasts.
(John of the Cross, *Spiritual Canticle* st. iii)

Alas, many people have quite a wrong idea of detachment.

It doesn't mean that I care nothing about the place I live in so long as I have food and shelter.

It doesn't mean that I take no interest in those I live with, that I let them get on with their lives while I get on with mine.

It doesn't mean that I pickle my heart in antiseptic lest I should be too fond of others or find myself overwhelmed with emotions of joy and sorrow.

It does mean however that my deep self is set upon pleasing God, so that I never allow these other things I care, and rightly care about — where I live, those I love — to usurp his place.

I say to the Lord, you are my God
My happiness lies in you alone. (Ps. 16, Grail)

I must never view means to God as ends in themselves, but bear to lose all for Jesus' sake. Each of us is called to virginity of soul, whether we are married or single. It is this spiritual virginity which delights the Lord's heart, and when given to him he is able to possess us with his own purity. This sounds grand of course, but in reality it can be a painful process — a lot of interior garbage has to be thrown onto the fire of God's love, and burning hurts!

Detachment has to be continually re-won. We break loose from one set of things only to be entangled by another set in which we initially thought to find freedom. It is a progressive leave-taking which is never complete, and this is reiterated everywhere. The woman must be separated from the child in her womb, then she must let him grow, walk, be educated, think his own thoughts, live his own life, walk away, while she continues her own personal journey with the Lord. Her love is fruitful only if it frees the other and frees her. But this is a costly business and few see it through.

The artist must leave his early attempts at self-expression and break out with courage into a new style if the vision in his heart is to be shared. It would be easier, safer, to concentrate on a few popular prints, clichés, but only at the price of personal growth.

The young nun must leave behind her first naive ideas of religious perfection, her love for externals, her understandable and praiseworthy attachment to those who have helped her, to enter into the real life-stream of the Church with its many human pains and problems.

If she does not she remains an adolescent and not a woman open to responsibility, sorrow, and mature Christian concern.

No one likes always to be making new beginnings, yet each time we 'begin' from a slightly different place. We have to keep making choices as we reach each new juncture of life. We have to detach ourselves, stand back, and endeavour to judge and choose in God's way, and not merely according to our own likes and dislikes. Self-giving has to be generous and wholehearted at each step, and then we shall see more clearly where we are still tied as slaves to self, where the bird inside us is unable to fly. We shall see the golden threads we are afraid to cut lest the bird escape from our control into the wide skies of God's life. We think that such exhilarating freedom would be too frightening to face. And we are right. We can only face it if we have, at each step, given ourselves to God, so we know at last that he can be trusted completely with all we are and have. Experience will have proved him as the tenderest of Fathers.

Detachment leads us unerringly to generosity and freedom. We give all because we know we shall receive all from the Lord. If we are only concerned to protect ourselves, our position, our friends, our belongings, we narrow ourselves down to their limits, and spiritual growth becomes impossible.

We need the detachment evidenced in the biblical Hannah, mother of Samuel — that little lad who no doubt fired our early imagination by his running back and forth to Eli to ascertain if the old priest had called him, and finally being told to respond, 'Speak Lord, thy servant is listening'. Sir Joshua Reynolds' plump 'child

Samuel at prayer' must have appeared on innumerable chocolate boxes and biscuit tins, bringing the incident to mind even if we could hardly identify with the long locks and creamy nightshirt.

Hannah was a woman for whom fulfilment lay in motherhood. Being a wife, even a greatly loved wife, loved 'more than seven sons', could not satisfy her longings. The woman who loves wants to bear children for her husband, for love must diffuse itself, both in the natural and spiritual sphere. So Hannah prays and entreats God for a child, and is heard. God blesses her with a son, whom she had previously promised to dedicate to his service. And what Hannah promised in affliction she fulfils in her joy. Her canticle of praise is the forerunner of Mary's Magnificat. The child is given to the Lord at great personal cost, for as yet she has no other children. Standing before Eli she says:

> 'This is the child I prayed for, and Yahweh granted me what I asked him. Now I make him over to Yahweh for the whole of his life. He is made over to Yahweh.' There she left him, for Yahweh.
>
> (I Sam. 1:27–8)

This selflessness, this offering of the precious one, is rewarded with an even more abundant fruitfulness for Hannah, and God takes the young Samuel as his prophet. Hannah is the model of human detachment, for she loves, but does not cling to what she loves.

Merely to have and hold on to what is good may thwart God's plan. We have to 'sell all and give to the poor' for his sake and the sake of the kingdom. For each, this 'selling all' takes a different form. We cannot decide, but we must hold ourselves in readiness, with the disposition to give God whatever he wants to have from us. Our hearts must be set on him — not on whether I have or have not, whether I go or stay. 'Give and it shall be given to you' is part of life's paradox.

The human heart seeks love. It longs to love and to be loved in return. And so we try to grab at love, we are afraid of losing out on it, of discovering ourselves to be unlovable. We want to keep our Samuel beside us. We are afraid that if we let people go we will lose them forever. Our 'love' is disguised selfishness and easily turns into a sour hatred. We want others to be exclusively ours when we have to let them be free. This applies in marriage, friendship and parental love. True freedom of heart is a lifelong struggle for most of us, but it leads to a universal love which is akin to the love of God himself. Our hearts are ultimately made for him, and if we want our human loves to be strong and selfless they must come under his influence. St Teresa points out (so truly!) that those who love 'in God', do so with a far more genuine passion than the counterfeit affection we so often mistake for the reality. True love of others is strengthened and purified when in it we seek nothing for ourselves.

If we reflect on our lives I'm sure this will be borne out by personal experience. Our real loves are the ones which free us; which have given, and continue to give us a greater ability to be ourselves, and to reach out to others, secure in love. We don't need to cling, for we know right to the marrow of our bones that 'love endures', physical separation has no power to divide what God has joined. I have discovered, through the tearing of my own heart, an inner expansion, by which not only the Lord enters the wound, but others too.

With him I find again those I love — more radiant, more free, more strong.

The detached heart is the heart that mirrors above all the tender heart of Jesus — not a heart of stony indifference but a heart of flesh, a new heart. We are quite wrong if we think of Jesus as unfeeling. He has all the best attributes of a sensitive human heart, he is wholly given, poured out, in love and devotion. Human love at its purest is an image of the divine. Mary's care for Elizabeth is the reflection of God's own care and concern.

When we love purely we live more fully, the world takes on a new beauty, we look upon everyone with kinder eyes.

And as we learn to let go of others so we learn to let go of all the accoutrements we have thought so essential to our self-esteem. We cease to worry what others think, we cease trying to impress. When God takes away some of our talents and leaves us in the shade we are able to remain at peace. When old age approaches with its decreasing powers and increasing disabilities we can accept these without resentment. We understand that in God we really *do* have everything, and we prove in our lives the verse St Teresa kept in her daily prayer book:

Nothing must disturb you,
nothing must affright you,
all things pass away.
God alone abideth
and with patient longing
make him your sole stay.
In him you have everything
hold to God and nought shall fail you.
He alone avails you.

Self and God

Mary travels to the hill country. As a mother she needs to discover herself in her new role in relationship with another woman who shares her calling. She still needs to be attuned spiritually to what she is physically.

Isn't this what life is about? A journey to become what we are. It is the development of the seed within us to its unique potential, its full flowering. We are all aware that we are not yet what we *could* be, what we are *called* to be.

For many people life just takes its course. 'Things happen' to them but they never actively control and respond to their destiny. They 'go to seed' as we say, and time shows them up as shallow, unfulfilled, stunted. For others the journey towards self-realisation, truth, happens slowly and painfully, but they have the courage to face up to reality when it presents itself. George Eliot, in her masterpiece *Middlemarch*, introduces us to Dorothea. She is a young woman who, in pursuing her 'dream' man, does not see in her idol what is obvious to those who look with unprejudiced vision. Dorothea bypasses the one who loves her and chooses instead a dull clergyman, Casaubon, whom she idealises, but who has in reality no depths, no inner capacity to call her forth in the way she so desperately desires. She marries a dream and ends up with a nightmare. Casaubon has not tried to deceive her, he is too unimaginative even for that — she has deceived herself. Yet Dorothea has the courage, when awakening comes, to assume her own responsibilities, to become the woman she was meant to be — and this at a far deeper level than if she had made no early mistakes.

The theme of personal discovery is perhaps easiest to depict in novels where we see people, as it were, from without *and* from within, and so we can gauge whether they are being true to life and to themselves. But in our own experience too we recognise that happiness lies only in being our 'true' self, which must be sought, however painful the search. A life's vocation is not something extraneous, superimposed from without; no, it is there from the beginning, intrinsic to our very existence. In finding our vocation we find God.

There is something utterly tragic about a wasted life, and it can happen to 'religious' people as much as to any others. So much early promise stagnates; we don't grow, we don't seek, we don't move on as Mary did. We settle down. And we don't see what is patently clear to others — we aren't *real*. We are stuffed dolls — like the whitened sepulchres Jesus refers to. We are all powder and paint on the outside, while inside, instead of functioning heart, lungs, liver, we are old bones, rags and rubbish. And we deceive no one but ourselves.

Human and spiritual growth demands absolute ruthlessness in seeking the truth and accepting the truth.

Much spiritual writing sounds poetic and uplifting because it evokes primal symbols, but love is never easygoing. The poetry of St John of the Cross' *Spiritual Canticle* masks a spirituality of the deepest demands.

We *need* poetry, it says more than we realise, but we only grow into it as we live it. Intellectual appreciation alone has no power to change us.

Love strips away all that is inauthentic in us. We cannot respond to a lie or a pretence in others, neither can they respond to the same in us. If we don't search for and come to terms with God and our inner self, a false self will take over. This is the self which is *not* made in God's image, is not vivified by the Spirit, and therefore has no power to awaken us to fullness of life and love. The choice is ours. Will we choose to reach out and find our true self in reality, in human relationships, in God; or shall we remain locked in our interior prison, surrounded by comforts which pall even as we pretend to enjoy them?

The Song of Songs, upon which the *Spiritual Canticle* is based, is the poetry of all poetry in the Bible. It is a treasure house of symbols for lovers. True love seeks, searches, mourns, rejoices, sorrows. . . . True love *lives*, and in the end is united with the object long sought and desired. Those who earnestly seek God will not be disappointed.

> On my bed, at night, I sought him
> whom my heart loves.
> I sought but did not find him.
> So I will rise and go through the City;
> in the streets and in the squares
> I will seek him whom my heart loves . . .
> . . . I found him . . .
> I held him fast, nor would I let him go.
>
> (S. of S. 3:1–4)

To have God is worth every sacrifice, all else pales in

comparison, and in finding him we find the love and fulfilment for which we were made. All our deepest yearnings in him are satisfied. But if we, through our own fault, refuse to move, to search, our lives are pathetically truncated. Here is an aspect of the paradox by which we must die to rise, accept pruning to further growth.

There is an urgency to our journey. Man's life is short in contrast to God's eternity; it is transitory and fragile.

A voice commands: 'Cry!'
and I answered, 'what shall I cry?'
— 'All flesh is grass
and it's beauty like the wild flower's . . .
The grass withers, the flower fades,
but the word of our God remains forever.'

(Isa. 40:6–7)

To recognise life's transitoriness is the beginning of wisdom — we develop a sense of due proportion. Only the fool behaves as if time will last forever.

For each of us comes 'our hour' when, like Jesus, we will either have finished, or not finished, the work we were given to do. This is indeed a key consideration in the passage from adolescence to adulthood . . . It is natural to want to make something of our lives, give them direction and purpose, and not fritter them away. Like St Thérèse we must cultivate a passionate desire to love God as fully as possible while the precious gift of time is ours.

Life is God's greatest gift to us and yet it is bounded by time in the form of the present moment. We shall only pass this particular way once, at this particular moment. What we do not say, do not do, remains forever unsaid, undone. The word of love, the deed of kindness, the opportunity missed, never returns — at least not in a precisely identical form.

Jesus stresses so much this preciousness. There is only today in which to trust the Father, to let him provide for us, while we seek him through loving and serving our neighbour. We have to seize the opportunities that lie at hand. *Now* is the time to find the treasure, to seek the pearl. *Now* is the time for wholeheartedness, total given-ness.

To live as a child is to live fully in the present. The goal of adulthood is to recapture that primal child. To be recollected has nothing to do with downcast eyes; recollection means living each moment wholly present to *whatever* we are doing. We have to be present to *every*thing and *every*one, not just to what we like, or to a few friends. Life must not be the span in which we *do* many things but *live* none of them.

In *Doctor Zhivago* the wondrous wholeness of Lara lies in her total presence to all she does. It is this which invests her with an aura of all-embracing beauty. She is present, recollected, whether nursing, studying, caring for her daughter, loving Yuri. She is never up-tight, tense, because she lives fully in the present. This is a major means of fostering balance, sanity — it keeps us from being overwhelmed by peripheral matters, useless worries. And it helps us too to live through periods of grief and pain, for we can never despair when we face each moment of life as a whole gift.

In the present we can always find God, even when circumstances appear unfavourable on the surface. Did not John of the Cross compose his great canticle during his imprisonment at Toledo, in the midst of loneliness and physical torment? Yet this is a song of the purest joy, because he knows God is with him:

My soul is occupied
and all my substance in his service.
Now I guard no flock.
Nor have I any other employment:
My sole occupation is love. (st. xxviii)

One who attains to wisdom in the knowledge of life's brevity, who gives all to God in the present moment, is led ultimately not to annihilation but to life in its fullness. The restless heart attains rest for it discovers the true self, the self known and loved by God before the beginning of the world.

Wounded for Glory

 A seeking love is a suffering love. Life's journey is not one of ease. To search for God, to search for our true self, is not a facile strolling. True love is suffering love. Why? Because we are naturally selfish, and to come close to another we have to break through painful barriers. If we go out to another, give ourselves in any way to another, we make 'the other' important, we expose ourselves to hurt, and this is painful for our ego. We are afraid we shall not live if our snail-shell is removed. Tenderly God takes the vulnerable, quivering little creatures we are in his hands; and his gentle 'wounding' awakens us to the wonder of life. We then feel bereft if God withdraws for a while; once we have experienced his touch we are forced to seek him with ever greater urgency.

> Why hast thou hidden thyself
> and left me to my sorrow, O my beloved.
> Thou hast fled like the hart
> having wounded me.
> I ran after thee crying but thou wast gone.
> (Spirtual Canticle st. i)

What is this wounding in the context of love, the

wounds John of the Cross speaks of as part of the seeker's pain?

Physical wounds are a lasting impression, an enduring mark, of suffering borne. On another level we speak of someone having been wounded in childhood, meaning that they bear the scars of rejection, ridicule. We speak of the wounds left by past experiences which seem to retard present growth. Nothing in our lives is as beautiful as we would wish it to be — we are only human beings after all, and not superpersons.

We tend therefore to look upon wounds as blemishes which diminish the completeness we *should* have, whereas in fact they can be positive assets. In fact, if we are to believe the insight of John of the Cross, God himself inflicts wounds upon us to *force* us out of our smug, self-satisfied life, so that we may be driven to seek him, and find in him ultimate healing and wholeness.

In the Bible, wounds are the ever-present sign of suffering love, the marks of love's anguish; they are attributed to God — our God is a wounded lover.

Those we love have a unique power to hurt us. We have only to consider how we react to the same snub when it comes from a mere acquaintance or from one who really matters to us. Divorce produces such terrible scars because a couple who were once close, two in one flesh, are prized apart amid bitter recriminations. Especially if one of the partners continues to love, persists in loving, the pain is intense — there is a rejection experienced which is like none other. And man in some analogous way has this power over God as the prophet Hosea tries to show. God is wounded by Israel's rejection of his proffered love; he is bewildered, hurt, if we can translate it into our halting human terminology.

I myself taught Ephraim to walk,
I took them in my arms;
yet they have not understood
that I was the one looking after them.
I led them with reins of kindness,
with leading-strings of love . . .
Israel, how could I give you up?.
My heart recoils from it. (Hos. 11:2,8)

In another passage Isaiah pictures God as having graven Jerusalem on the palms of his hands. He has marked himself with a continuous reminder of his faithful love. His people matter to him (Isa. 49:16).

It is the same in literature. Love, if it is worthy of the name, costs something, or rather, everything. A great love story, like that of Romeo and Juliet, moves the hearts of the world. But human love is only a shadow of the great love of God for men. God gives us all in his Son, and he wants us to make a total response.

Love which is unable or unwilling to suffer is merely a form of disguised selfishness. The Church's liturgy makes much of the wounding of Christ, placing on his lips the words of the prophet Zechariah: 'These wounds I received in the house of my friends' (Zech. 13:6). The early Fathers see the wounded heart, pierced to become a fountain, opened up to cleanse sin and impurity. The heart of Jesus is the symbol of costly, suffering love, the source of grace. In exposing his heart Christ has his side opened, like Adam, to espouse his new bride, the Church. Doubting Thomas has the Lord point to his wounds as the proof of his living reality. In the heavenly kingdom his wounds endure: he is the slain Lamb, ever living and interceding for men.

A woman too expresses her love by bearing pain willingly. She longs to take the sufferings of her child, her beloved, upon herself. Love and suffering are inseparably linked. But while God's love is totally pure, ours is selfish. We are always thinking 'What is in this for me?' We must be brought to suffering to prove our love and break out of self. A woman must know the pain of childbearing before she holds her child in her arms — in 'losing' herself in some way, she gains another. It is the same in our relationship with God.

> The soul loses itself, making no account whatever of itself, but of the Beloved, resigning itself freely into his hands without any selfish views, losing itself deliberately and seeking nothing for self. . . . Such is he that loves God; he seeks neither gain nor reward but only to lose all, even himself, according to God's will.
> (*Spiritual Canticle* st. xxix)

God is the inflictor of wounds so that we may eventually enter into a lasting convenant with him, stripped of all pride. Then we may bear children of faith for the Church, trusting not in ourselves but in him who makes us fecund. And as God wounds us, so he is the one who soothes the sore — and only he, for: 'there can be no remedy for the wounds of love but from him who inflicted them. And so the wounded soul runs after the Beloved, crying to him for relief' (*Spiritual Canticle* st. i). The timid child, the scarred being within us, must be brought under the healing touch of God, who has permitted our sorrow in order to draw us to himself.

What then are the wounds of love? They are certainly not wounds of great longing for God in the realm of feeling; if they were, then most of us would have to say

regretfully that we had never experienced them. No, they are merely the wounds of ordinary life: our difficulties of temperament — flaring anger, melancholy, or too great ebullience; character defects — moodiness, inability to adapt, instability; all the hurts of past and present — our longing for affection, our lost childhood, our broken marriage perhaps, the bearing of loneliness and sorrow, all that seems to make us persons who are partial and incomplete.

Life demands that we grow through all these to a deeper trust in God. In fact the healing of our deepest brokenness can only be his work.

> Come let us return to Yahweh.
> He has torn us to pieces but he will heal us;
> he has struck us down, but he will bandage our
>   wounds. (Hos. 6:1,2)

By accepting the reality of incompleteness we are brought to see how little we can do ourselves. We are not self-sufficient. The Almighty alone can work marvels for us — his Name is holy, not ours. And as the wounds of Christ in heaven are the permanent signs of his love, so our own life's wounds can become our glory, for they force us into his loving arms.

If we question ourselves closely we surely see it is our wounds, our unique experience of life's sorrows, that form us as individuals, able to give God praise. We know each other, too, far more surely by our weaknesses than by our strengths, and so we are led from self-sufficiency to community, to a love based on reality and not illusion.

Of course there is nothing magical about the healing process we have to go through so that life's wounds don't fester and become merely a source of bitterness rather than stepping stones to God. Turning to him for conversion (healing) is only a beginning and not an end; it is a continuous process.

> In all these dangers and strugglings and others like them you see the shuddering of my heart. I feel not so much that I do not suffer from my wounds as that they are being healed by you time and time again.
>
> (St Augustine, *Confessions* X:39)

Healing, like wounding, comes to us mainly through others and through life. There is a continuous alternation of both which are the effects of God's touch, coming to us, if we use our faith, through daily interaction, daily understanding. These will always be opening up new depths within us and new capacities for response.

But ultimately we must remember that no one but God can make us whole. We cannot force the process, only accept it. However, we *can* be open to others, risking the pain of self-exposure, making room for God to come in.

Above all we must never despair. *Anything* in our life can be a wound of love; any suffering, any diminishment, any painful memory, any neurosis, as long as we open it to God and to men. The psalms especially will begin to take on new meaning as we express pain, sorrow, longing, bewilderment, joy, as each step of our life unfolds beneath God's gaze.

In the end we shall come to understand that our sufferings have been as it were the very cause of our coming to life. The 'little snail' has found a new home in the temple of God.

O sweet burn,
O delicious wound,
O tender hand! O gentle touch,
savouring of everlasting life
and paying the whole debt.
By slaying thou hast changed death into life.

                (John of the Cross, *Living Flame*)

A Heart of Compassion

A woman who entered deeply into the mystery of the wounded Christ, the enigma of sin, and the Christian vocation as a personal search, was Julian of Norwich, who spent most of her life drawing out the meaning of her *Revelations* in the anchorhold of St Julian's Church in that city. There is very little that we know about Julian's personal history — not her name, nor her place of birth — and yet on another plane we feel we *do* know her, as a dedicated, common-sense woman struggling with the doctrines of Christianity, the woman who cannot help emerging from her writings.

I wonder sometimes if she came originally from the coast, for we know of her mysterious vision of the sea-bed (*Rev.* ch. 10), unusual for an inland dweller. And what of her comparison of the drops of blood spreading out under the thorn crown 'like the scales of herring' (ch. 7)? Herrings are a sea fish and not to be found in Norfolk rivers. Perhaps she even knew the sands of Blakeney which can be seen from the north side of our present Carmel, the horizon disappearing beyond an expanse of grey water. . . .

Julian most certainly comes into the mainstream of the English mystical tradition, with Walter Hilton and the author of *The Cloud*, and she lived at a time when the solitary life was held in high honour. But although I am not a scholar I find in Julian several traits which, for me, locate her spirituality in the line of the béguines of Europe; and it is interesting to note that after her death two béguinages were actually established in Norwich, the *only* city in England to be so honoured. Norfolk has always been specially associated with the Low Countries where the béguines originated, and it is by no means impossible that their spirit was transmitted to Julian through the many friars, Franciscan, Dominican, Carmelite, who had houses in the county, and who, abroad, were so closely connected with the whole movement as spiritual directors.

The béguine phenomenon was essentially feminine in origin: it comprised women bound by no vows, no official Rule, no central government. It was a life of simple dedication to God either in a community or in one's own home — often coupled with works of mercy — and it gave scope for free, independent piety apart from the vowed religious way. The movement rose to rapid popularity in the thirteenth century but it also had its detractors, and in 1312 the béguines were officially proscribed at the Council of Vienne. They still continued in many places, however, even though some communities sought to ally themselves with established Orders. Evidence of their popularity is found in 1455 when the Ten Elsem béguines (Netherlands) were affiliated to the Carmelites, and the Norwich béguinages date from around the same time. It was certainly a movement which did much to offer women a certain independence, especially if they were of middle-class origin and might not have sufficient dowry for a

monastic establishment, yet were too well educated to be lay sisters in the same.

Now it seems to me that when we look at Julian we see many traces of béguine influence. She is almost certainly a middle-class woman; she is living at home, presumably in a dedicated way of life at the time of her visions; she writes in the vernacular, typical of the béguines who were not Latin-trained as were nuns; she exhibits a deep personal love of the wounded Saviour and his mother which is at the heart of the mendicant tradition; there is in her writings nothing of the excesses of penitential discipline — she is 'homely' in the best sense, she is an 'even-Christian' rather than one of the élite. It is surely possible therefore that through the Norfolk friars she was cognisant of the béguine tradition, and that they disseminated that spirit among women who sought their direction. Most interesting it seems are the Carmelite foundations at Burnham Norton and Blakeney on the coast,[1] for this Order has a tradition of solitude and its Rule is based on the eremitical life. Carmelites also had a house in Norwich and were known to give individuals direction in the solitary life even though they had no established communities of women. If Julian had spiritual ties with the béguine movement would it not also help to explain why her vernacular writing on personal revelations were held suspect, and not popularised until many years later?

However, speculation aside, I would like to look at one aspect of Julian's teaching. She tells us that she asked for the gift of three wounds; the wounds of contrition, compassion, and longing for God. She saw these as something *all* can desire without reservation, and it is in treating of compassion that Julian shows herself most a woman. She has in mind particularly compassion for the Lord, an entering into his suffering with fellow-feeling, but as the *Revelations* progress this widens to include *all* men, her 'even-Christians'. In fact

[1]Founded 1241 and 1296 respectively.

46

without the wound of compassion we are incomplete human beings, a whole dimension of life is missing:

> I saw how Christ has compassion upon us because of our sins. And just as previously I had been full of sorrow and compassion at the sight of his suffering, so now I was filled with compassion for my fellow Christians. . . . I saw that all the kind compassion and love a man may have for (them) is due to the fact that Christ is in him. (*Rev.* ch. 28)

What is compassion? It is the ability to enter into the mind and heart of another, to share his sorrow, to know him 'from within', thus giving rise to mercy and understanding. It is one of the attributes of God in the Old Testament, it is the practical way he manifests his steadfast love, for he understands man's weakness (Lam. 3:32). The psalmist sings that God is tender to the despised, the sorrowful — slow to anger, good to all, compassionate to all his creatures, he raises those who are bowed down. In these and similar words we see the feminine attributes of God as Mother, caressing and caring for her beloved people: 'Like a son comforted by his mother will I comfort you' (Isa. 66:13).

Genesis makes it perfectly clear that the image of God is a combination of masculine and feminine; and the response on our part to such a totality of love must be, can only be, absolute trust: 'As a child rests on its mother's knee, so I place my soul in your loving care' (Ps. 130). In the New Testament how often we read that Jesus had compassion (literally, 'was moved by the bowels of yearning') for the sick, the erring, for the sheep without shepherd, for all forms of human misery.

He took no thought for himself when he saw others in need.

Julian makes much of Jesus as mother because of his practical caring. Like a mother, she says, Jesus nourishes us with his word and his body, bringing us to new birth in God:

> This fine and lovely word *Mother* is so sweet and so much its own that it cannot properly be used of any but him, and of her who is his own true Mother — and ours. In essence *motherhood* means love and kindness, wisdom, knowledge, goodness.
>
> (*Rev.* ch. 60)

And Jesus too identifies himself with the hen who wants to gather her chicks beneath her wing ('but *you* would not'). His is the cry of wounded love, of a mother whose children refuse help and insist on their own ruin. A mother suffers for her children *because* she loves them. She cannot but be compassionate.

The heart of a mother reflects the heart of God, and we should be slow to shrug this off with the statement, 'it's only natural'. Julian we may note asked specifically for the wound of *natural* (kind) compassion — not some rarefied spiritual gift but a flowering of what God has implanted in our very natures if we know ourselves aright.

In any case, is such love natural as *opposed* to God-like? Not at all! It is the enfleshment of the love of the Lord, who loves creatively as does a mother. What is weak, imperfect, unformed, he loves into being, thereby making it lovable. It is not a matter of the Perfect One loving the perfect creature, but goodness and self-giving reaching out to the imperfect and partial — as to a baby who is not yet a person but has to become one.

This mother love is the model for our own. The mother does not love only her good children, but *all* her children, and for no other reason than that they are hers; she has borne them and so she sees them with the eyes of her heart. In our relationships we need to exercise our heart muscles which, alas, are all too often stiff from lack of use. St Thérèse, that truly community minded saint, within her limited cloistered world hit on this love as the centre of relational life. We are not to love merely those who please us, but to go out to those who are defective, uncongenial, unsympathetic perhaps to our views. Then, as with a mother, the warmth of given love brings forth a response of love, even in the weakest, opening the way for real growth.

Like Thérèse we must really open ourselves to those we live with, accept them as God's gift, search out and nurture all that is fine in them; then they will cease to be a burden for they will be secure in our hearts. We should not be satisfied with loving *all* at a level which is really the lowest common denominator we can find: 'I'll love everyone a little, then I'll be quite safe, clean, above reproach, "charitable".' No, we must be always striving to love to our greatest capacity, taking as our measure those we love truest and deepest.

Julian calls compassion a wound. It is so because human experience teaches us that if we love we suffer. It's therefore easier not to love, for if we do we give the other power to hurt us. The pains of those we love become our own, and the more we love the more we open ourselves to possible rejection with its attendant emotions. If we love we 'feel' for others, and the more we widen our hearts to include all, the more we shall find ourselves bearing the sorrows of the world — as Mary carried Jesus within her to bring him forth for the destiny of the Cross. 'You too will be pierced to the heart, that out of *many* hearts thoughts may be revealed' (Luke 2:35).

In her anchorite cell Julian may have been unable to *do* much, but she could lend a listening ear, an understanding spirit — these are needed above all. There is nothing judgemental in her writings. She never sees herself as set apart from others, either for good or bad. She is one in Christ with all those who share with her in the parish Eucharist; one with those who come to her black-curtained window with the recluse's white cross embroidered on it; one with the miller, the priest, the housewife — those whose sorrows and joys she must have shared in her years of seclusion.

And the confidence God gave Julian she desired to communicate to all. She hoped that they too, through knowing the love of Christ crucified, would turn to their neighbour with a like glance of pity and compassion, and know *each one* to be clothed in the goodness and mercy of God. Hers is no depressing spirituality. We have only to read the *Revelations* to see how Julian's life was one of homely joy. She understood that God's amazing love *is* his meaning, and so, even though wounded, we have nothing to be afraid of. All shall be well.

The Blossoming Desert

 As we mature in God's ways our early self-satisfaction decreases. We see that much of what we thought was virtue was merely youthful good spirits, good health or, worse, a pious priggishness which claimed to know all the answers. Fortunately God doesn't face us too soon with our worst side, but one day it *must* be faced if we are to grow up and leave childish ways behind us.

It has been said that to attain purity of heart (which is ultimately a single-minded direction towards God) is the aim of the Christian — to be completely Christ-ed. *Everything* must lead us to the Father, as it did Jesus. 'To the pure all things are pure.' God alone is the wellspring of our blessedness and our joy.

The path to purity of heart is self-knowledge, and the two must grow apace. Without the love of God we cannot know the self we should love, and only God can enable us to accept ourselves just as we are, without pretence, without masks, without self-recrimination or despair. But strangely enough self-knowledge is not the product of a lot of introspection and journal writing, though these may help. It comes from associating with others, as St Teresa points out in the masterly fifth chapter of her *Book of Foundations*. Teresa is writing for her nuns who are vowed to a life of solitude and prayer, yet she says the battle for self-knowledge is fought through human interaction, hence no one should wish to avoid the knocks and rubs of community living. We can all think we are virtuous, prayerful, God-centred . . . when we are alone! But let us find ourselves in situations with others and we quickly see that we are mistaken; our so-called perfection comes to grief! And what is more, when we then *do* get time to ourselves the bad moments of failure keep repeating in our minds like lumps of undigested food.

So we get discouraged, perhaps self-pitying. But Teresa then shows the remedy for this self-disgust — look at our Lord. From him we will learn true humility; from gazing at his goodness and beauty rather than our ugliness we will be encouraged to go on, to trust him who came not to call the righteous (which we were so sure of being) but sinners (which we now know we are). Self-knowledge is absolutely basic to a life of prayer, it is our daily bread, but it is not a bitter bread for love makes all things sweet.

Julian writes:

I saw that for our perfection we must have a desire to know our soul with wisdom and accuracy. This will teach us to look for it where in fact it is, in God. And so by the gracious guidance of the Holy Spirit we come to know them both together. (*Rev.* ch. 56)

What a beautiful word 'wisdom' is, and in the Bible it is depicted as so penetrating, pure and gentle. As our soul is 'enclosed in God' so we can rely on him to lead us surely to a proper understanding of who we are, at each stage of growth revealing more to us, in the manner of a mother who helps her child to attain ever greater directed-ness.

Often though it seems we are in a desert, that the promised land of God is just too remote, and that it would be better to forget about it and return to base. We forget that the desert experience is part of life; we cannot journey all the time through paradisal surroundings if we are to be stretched to bear God for the world.

The desert saw the birth travail of Israel, and from it she emerged as a people. For us too there must be a similar period before we can be reborn as the people God meant us to be. The seed of Christ's inner life was hidden until it flowered at the Resurrection, revealing the glory within; and we 'die' in him to the superficial self to discover our true identity. We come to depend on him for everything, realising our own inadequacy and the unlimited mercy of God. No matter how much others may help us we must ultimately face our solitude, and in it we find the mystery of God — we realise like Israel of old that we needed suffering so as fully to appreciate joy.

> . . . Do not forget Yahweh your God who brought you out of the land of Egypt, out of the house of slavery: who guided you through this vast and dreadful wilderness . . . who in this waterless place brought you water . . . who in this wilderness fed you with manna . . . to humble you and test you and so make your future the happier. (Deut. 8:14–16)

But even as we press on we find we do not have to wait for fulfilment. The desert itself blossoms, symbol of the Lord's presence, a sign of his love and predilection.

In the wilderness I will put cedar trees,
acacias, myrtles, olives.
In the desert I will plant juniper,
plane tree and cypress side by side:
so that men may know and understand
that the hand of Yahweh has done this.

(Isa. 41:19, 20)

Our desert poverty and dependence are precisely what call forth God's mercy; we face our neediness and lack of resources, and yet keep on trusting that if we have faith he will let all things blossom into joy.

When I was a schoolgirl I spent some time being educated in Germany at a comprehensive school for British Army children located in Wilhelmshaven on the north coast. It was more than ten years since the end of World War II but Wilhelmshaven was still a devastated town. At weekends when we walked round the place there were piles of rubble waiting to be cleared, great grey bunkers cracked and yawning empty; across the Fliegerdyke were rows of wooden huts where families lived in utter poverty, frozen by the winter winds that whipped across the sea and clogged the bay with ice-floes. And yet, in the midst of barrenness we would suddenly come upon patches of cleared ground, marked out, tilled, and green with vegetables, pansies, seedlings of all kinds and those enormous sunflowers which seem to be the pride of every German who can put spade to soil. These little oases were true signs of hope, gladdening to the heart; the desert of Wilhelmshaven was blooming.

So it is with us. Even at the very time all seems hopeless our desert suddenly takes on a new look: God

makes his presence felt perhaps by the smile of a friend, a fleeting handclasp and whispered 'I love you', an unexpected letter of encouragement or even such a small thing as being down in the dumps and then finding our favourite biscuits are on the supper table. God uses others to lighten our pathway just as he uses us to lighten theirs. And often it is the very people who forced us to see our weak side who now show us that under- neath we *are* loved and accepted, and so we can love and accept ourselves and believe that God too loves and accepts us just as we are. It is the working of that wisdom which is 'so pure, she invades and permeates all things . . .'

She is a reflection of the eternal light,
untarnished mirror of God's active power,

image of his goodness. . . .
herself unchanging, she makes all things new. . . .
She deploys her strength from one end of the earth
  to the other,
ordering all things for good. (Wisd. 7:24–8:1)

Inner Wisdom, the Spirit of God, helps us to realise that the desert is not there for itself, it is there as a route into the Promised Land. As John of the Cross points out in the *Spiritual Canticle*, God takes care of the one traversing the desert — she is as a bird placed in his hands, and, taking pity on its loneliness, he has 'taken care of it, held it in his arms, fed it with all good things, and guided it to the deep things of God'.

Like Mary we set out from the sweetness and familiarity of our Galilee to go into the desert country of Judea. But once we have arrived, at home once more in new surroundings, we can burst into song — a new song that gathers up our past and sees us into a new redemptive future.

Fruitful in Surrender

Mary sings, 'My soul glorifies the Lord, my spirit rejoices in God my Saviour.' She is the new bride of Yahweh, saved by him and given meaning in him, just as in the ancient world a husband rescued his wife from anonymity and gave her love, security, fecundity.

Brideship symbolises a culminating point in a woman's life. She loses her individual status to conjoin with another, and yet she is made even more herself for love opens up new depths in her. The bride stands alone on her wedding day as *the* loved one, she is radiant *because* she is loved — not in general but in particular. The image of the soul as bridge is in the purest biblical tradition. To be surrendered to God, made one with him in mutual self-giving, is the end of the spiritual journey and the beginning of the song of eternity.

In the desert Israel became the betrothed of Yahweh through the covenant; she promised to belong to him alone.

> 'I remember the affection of your youth,
> the love of your bridal days:
> you followed me through the wilderness,
> through a land unsown.' (Jer. 2:2)

When we read of the Virgin Israel this is not a term of

praise as many think; she is Israel left to her own devices so that she learns by bitter experience that only in Yahweh, her husband, has she meaning and fruitfulness.

> How can I describe you, to what compare you,
> daughter of Jerusalem?
> who can rescue and comfort you
> virgin daughter of Sion?
> For huge as the sea is your affliction;
> who can possibly cure you? (Lam. 2:13)

God, reducing Israel to poverty (virginity), does so only that he may wed her anew. He is *always* faithful to his choice of her.

> I did forsake you for a brief moment,
> but with great love I will take you back. (Isa. 54:6)

> Like a young man marrying a virgin,
> so will the one who built you wed you,
> and as the bridegroom rejoices in his bride
> so will your God rejoice in you. (Isa. 62:4–5).

In receiving Israel back, God reclothes her in the bridal garments of redemption, and promises that her union with him will result in the gift of progeny. Her barrenness will be taken away as was Sarah's of old (Isa. 51:2,3).

Israel in her chosen-ness prefigures Mary, Bride of the Spirit, joyful mother of the Church. As the virgin daughter of Sion Mary embodies the good tidings brought to the poor. She is the woman sought out and loved, therefore she proclaims God's mercy 'from generation to generation'. Mary is the model of the Christian soul, an image of the undivided, bridal love *all* should have for the Lord. She reveals the intimacy into which Christians are called, whatever their walk of life. She belongs to the Lord, body and soul.

In the Eucharist the Body of Christ is given for the bride-Church, the bride-Christian: 'My body . . . for you' — as the husband is 'for' his beloved through his body. God in his turn does not want us to respond to him with something outside ourselves — 'sacrifices and oblations' — no, he wants what he has given me as *me*: my body, my flesh.

Jesus' self-offering to the Father, which involved the continual accomplishment of the Father's will, was worked out in his own body, and likewise it must be worked out in ours. By his body, born of Mary, sacrificed on the Cross, risen and glorious, he opened for us a path to follow which leads ultimately to bliss; and we go to the Father through his body and our own. 'I give Christ my body to make up what is still to be suffered', sings St Paul. My body, my whole flesh, all of me — this is what dedication means. *All* of me: not some part only, not what I would have liked to have been and failed to be, not merely what I think or feel or say. And this gift of our flesh means complete self-donation: an acceptance of all that we are, all we have made ourselves, all that others have done to us — the material aspects of our life, environment, family, friends and so-called 'enemies' — all that is part of the complex being I know to be myself.

Our initial self-gift is worked out through the sign and symbol of sacrament. God comes to us through the material elements of life; his Flesh touches my flesh to make me a complete person rooted in the mystery of the Incarnation. My response to the Incarnate Love of

God in Christ can only be a bridal offering of myself
— *all* of myself — so that the seed of predestination,
divined darkly, is nurtured to blossom in wholeness and
integrity. *All* of me must be exposed to the light of God;
the good, the bad; the shame and guilt I feel as well as
the joy; my natural gifts of affection, my senses and
emotions. Nothing is hidden, nothing glossed over, thus
I stand in the truth.

A love that is willing to stand before God just as it
is makes Christianity *real*, thorough going. It issues in
a lived fidelity, so that I truly become God's temple
upon earth, the reflection of his Son who lives anew in
me. By looking at him, living with him, I catch his
beauty, and by what I become show all the world that
Jesus is living in his Church — not living in my spirit
alone but incarnated in my very flesh. 'When the truth
shines out in the soul', says St Bernard, 'and the soul
sees itself in the truth, there is nothing more impressive
than that testimony. And when the splendour of this
beauty fills the entire heart it naturally becomes visible
. . . Shining out like rays upon the body it makes it a
mirror of itself, so that its beauty appears in a man's
every action, his speech, his looks, his movements and
his smile' (*Sermon on the Song of Songs* 85).

Conformity to Christ is the end of all dedication to
him. And love? This is proved by a fidelity which must
be deepened and strengthened over the years. Love
endures — this is what St Paul points out. It does not
pass when emotions dry up, it does not rest in the
sweetness of my awakening to God in childhood or
early youth, nor in the thought that I have known what
it is to be engraced. Rather, I must be stretched painfully
to accommodate more love — to know Christ crucified,

which is what love is actually about — conformity to the Beloved. Be faithful, singlehearted, to this Teresa of Avila returns continually in her writings; let God work in you. And we know it is possible because God himself is faithful. The Father's love, as delineated by the prophet Hosea, the love of bridegroom for bride, is unchangeable, sacred, intimate, enduring and tender. This is the love Jesus enfleshed as he spoke in his last discourse before going forth to his Passion, when he freely laid down his life, loving to the end.

What is it that threatens our love, makes it weak and faltering? Our love is not the love spoken of in the Song of Songs that 'no waters avail to quench, no floods to drown', the love that is rooted and grounded upon the rock of Christ and trust in him. We let ourselves be too quickly overwhelmed by unruly passions, self-seeking, self-pity. The sufferings of life which come to us through circumstances, through others, through weakness of character, all that goes to make up our life 'in the flesh' we use as excuses for not growing, not risking. We don't want to be hurt.

But the message of Jesus is that suffering need not diminish us as persons; in fact, without a certain measure of suffering we cannot reach an enduring love at all. What does he know who has never been tested? Rather, we have to learn to open ourselves to the waters of suffering; in this way they will not destroy us but cleanse us, nurture and cradle us, like the child waiting to be born from the dark waters of the womb. We must 'go with' all that life brings us in the way of pain, misunderstanding, sorrow. We must go courageously into these waters that our love may be strengthened, not swept away. Let us be, as John of the Cross says in the *Dark Night*, hidden and protected in the dark waters close to God, for in them God is tabernacled, and in them the soul finds strength to endure.

So, let us be glad that we have been called and chosen for close union with the Lord, and realise that nothing is wasted when we surrender to his love. Like Abraham and Sarah we will give birth to a multitude:

Consider Abraham your father
and Sarah who gave you birth.
For he was alone when I called him,
but I blessed and increased him.
Yes, Yahweh has pity on Sion . . .
turns her desolation into an Eden,
her wasteland into the garden of Yahweh.
Joy and gladness shall be found in her,
thanksgiving and the sound of music. (Isa. 51:2–3)

All is His Gift

 While we may meditate on God's choice of his people in bridal love, we seem to get a better picture of our own state if we look at the nuptial allegory depicted in chapter 16 of the prophet Ezekiel.

Ezekiel begins his narrative with Israel as a new-born child, unwashed, uncared for, left struggling naked in her birth blood. And it is on this unwanted child that God has pity. He bids the tiny waif to live, and she grows to beautiful, natural maidenhood. God then takes this young woman under his wing; he spreads his cloak about her as a gesture of marriage, and he enters into a covenant of love with her. She develops into a queen — regal, elegant, crowned and bedecked with jewels by her divine Lover, all the finest food and raiment are at her disposal. Her fame spreads and she is renowned for her splendour. But this queen of queens turns wanton, prostitutes herself to others, shows a base ingratitude. All that can happen now is for her to be returned to her shameful initial state — more shameful because it is not a natural progression but one brought about by violence and disgrace. Israel, like us, learns humility from humiliation. Yet at the end of the chapter we see that indeed the gifts and call of God are not revoked. He takes back his humbled, chastened bride, re-establishing the covenant in such a way that Israel can no longer glory in anything of her own, but only in the pure, tender mercy of God who has loved her first.

In this we see the truth of the Lord's words in Deuteronomy 'it was not because you were great that he chose you but simply because he loved you' (Deut. 7:7). There is no room for self-trust. On reading Ezekiel's story do we not discern much of our own life's pattern? Each of us has to learn that all depends on God — there is no merit of ours in his choice, his grace, rather we were chosen not for our merit but for our helplessness. We are not 'worthy' any more than Israel of old was worthy.

> I saw you struggling in your blood as I was passing, and I said to you as you lay in your blood: Live, and grow like the grass of the fields. . . . Then . . . your time had come, the time for love. I spread part of my cloak over you and covered your nakedness; I bound myself by oath, I made a covenant with you, it is the Lord Yahweh who speaks — and you became mine. I bathed you in water . . . I anointed you with oil, I gave you embroidered dresses. . . . The fame of your beauty spread through the nations because I had clothed you with my own splendour. (Ezek. 16:6–14)

There is no answer to the mystery of Christian vocation except as a response to love. 'You did not return affection for affection but anticipated all love', says St Bernard.

But we so easily prostitute our gifts, we compromise, not necessarily as a deliberate affront to God but because we are fallible human beings. Fortunately for us we cannot just sail ahead like Spanish galleons laden with the bullion of virtues and talents. Every now and then God lets us be overwhelmed, appear 'failures', and what a blessing this is! Once we taste our weakness we stop preening ourselves. We have our temperamental good points and we accept them as our 'right' — our cheerfulness (and then life's pain touches us), our silence (and then we find ourselves gossiping unkindly), our patience (and suddenly we blow up). All we can do is run back into God's arms and start all over again.

The first covenant God enters into with us is a beginning, not an end. In speaking of this passage in Ezekiel John of the Cross points out that perfection is a progressive work (*Spiritual Canticle* st. xxiii). We have to keep moving forward whereas we too easily trust and rest in what *has* been given. We want a marriage in which we are not violated, and so we miss out on the real joys in store for those who surrender freely to love.

We are all faithless brides, but God is always at hand, waiting in the wings as it were for us to come back to him. To be stripped and humbled is as much part of life as being adorned. I feel that each of us would recognise ourselves in these sentences from the hand of a spiritual master:

> . . . The soul learns the reality of its misery . . . for in the day of festivity, when it found great sweetness, comfort and help in God, it was highly satisfied and pleased, thinking that it rendered God some service. . . . But when it has put on the garments of heaviness, of aridity and abandonment, when its previous lights have become darkness, it possesses and retains more truly that excellent and necessary

virtue of self-knowledge, counting itself for nothing, and having no satisfaction in itself because it sees that of itself it can do nothing.

(John of the Cross, *Dark Night*)

God chooses the weak things of the world to confound the strong. His choice is a deep mystery, and it demands our response most especially when he lets us feel our absolute need of his strength, and our own inability to adorn ourselves.

It we look at Rembrandt's painting, 'The Jewish Bride', we see an image of mature, humble love. There is no self-display, just unutterable trust and tenderness. The partner's hands meet over the woman's breast as her other hand strays to her womb to signify fruitfulness. This woman knows she will be loved through thick and thin and she gazes wonderingly into the distance as she ponders the mystery of it all.

Place your hand — so,
Let me feel the feeling you have for my own heart
So hard to my own touch
Which dares not to nest there
Fearful of finding it soften, quivering.

Be it soft to your touch
Its secrets unfolding, held in your confidence,
And there let mine rest and
·Knowing nothing to fear
Hold fast my own heart, owned and embraced.

(Jean Vials)

Many years ago now I saw a film on the life of St Bernadette. As with all productions of this kind a certain amount of fictitious licence is inevitable.

However, one part struck me forcibly. It may not have been true in itself, but there was certainly a true insight behind it. Bernadette has finished her education and is staying on as a boarder with the Sisters of Charity in the Lourdes hospice. One day the bishop comes to visit, and taking Bernadette aside he asks whether, now she is a young lady, she has given any thought to her future. With delightful simplicity Bernadette replies that well . . . she hasn't really . . . she had just been thinking perhaps a little home, a family of her own . . . she has no definite plans. The bishop looks at her wisely: 'No, Bernadette', he says, 'this isn't possible. Heaven has chosen you, now *you* must choose heaven.' And I feel that this is basic to any committed Christian vocation. God's choice of us must evoke a reciprocal choice on our part (even if ways of following it out differ). 'I *chose* Jesus to be my heaven', says Julian of Norwich, and this is lived out, enfleshed in our daily lives. Choosing Jesus, choosing heaven, is not a once for all thing, even though we might have known a decisive hour in the past. It is a *continual* choice, involving body, mind and heart, an alternation of adornment and stripping, which proves that our love is real and faithful, enduring to death and beyond.

> . . . for richer for poorer
> in sickness and in health
> in bad times and good
> for time and for eternity.

Witnesses to Grace

 In the ancient (and modern) world of violence and social upheaval the darkness is pierced by two woman who carry within themselves the destiny of their race — Ruth and Esther. They are lamps which cannot be hidden beneath a bushel; the pure light they cast is a light which fills the Church with the glowing flames of devotion and courage. Ruth is the 'true bride' who shelters beneath the wings of Yahweh, Esther the queenly intercessor for her people. Both women are images of the Christian who responds fully to each moment as it unfolds.

Ruth is a very short biblical book with no direct reference made to God in it. It *seems* to be a domestic narrative, but underneath the surface runs the beautiful theme of 'hesed' — faithful love — love of God mirrored in human love. There is something here with which all can identify; there are no extraneous wonders, no marvels, no prophetic voices, yet the Lord is at work in and through relationships, weaving his canvas of salvation history in the family life of a young foreign girl and her mother-in-law.

In Ruth we see 'hesed' from the human angle. She is a woman who, by her rock-like fidelity, depicts the soul who clings to the Lord. 'Let us go both together Lord', writes Teresa of Avila, 'wherever you go I will go, and by whatever way you pass I will follow.' This is of course an adaptation of Ruth's immortal words as she addresses Naomi, begging to be allowed to remain with her, to share her life, to go with her into the unknown:

'Wherever you go, I will go
wherever you live, I will live.
Your people shall be my people,
and your God, my God.
Wherever you die, I will die
and there I will be buried.
May Yahweh do this thing to me
and more also,
if even death should come between us!'

(Ruth 1:16–17)

Orpah, ordinary goodness and common sense personified, returns to her own people, but not Ruth; she faces the future with exemplary trust, determined to be faithful at whatever cost. And so God can use Ruth. She chooses him (though she does not know it) in choosing the path of generous devotion to Naomi.

Ruth is in fact the feminine equivalent of Abraham; she goes forth from her own kindred and country to a people and a God unknown to her. She is sustained by no divine promise, and yet her action is rewarded. She who elected, out of love, an almost certain barrenness (Ruth 1:12) is destined to be the great-grandmother of David, forerunner of the Messiah. Through Ruth *all* the peoples of the earth are blessed. In joining herself initially to Naomi with filial devotion she is joined to Naomi's people; she consents to share their fate and their destiny, as a woman embarking on marriage or religious life consents to share the unknown that lies

69

ahead with her new family or her new community.
Loyalty to others is a prerequisite, and yet in joining
ourselves with them we paradoxically become more
individual. Ruth's personality is enriched, not impover-
ished. Throughout the story she advances in stature,
from daughter-in-law to lover, wife and mother. She is
a source of blessing to all with whom she comes in
contact. Prepared for labour and hardship she finds rest
and bliss.

John of the Cross likens the soul to Ruth in its
relationship with God. Just as Ruth captured the heart
of Boaz by her silent fidelity, her trust in his honourable
intent, his suitability to be her husband and her
'redeemer' (Ruth 3:7–11), so the soul may silently and
trustfully approach the Lord and hope for divine union:

I will draw near to thee in silence and uncover thy
feet that thou mayest unite me to thyself making my
soul thy bride. I will rejoice in nothing till I am in
thy arms. O my God, I beseech thee, leave me not
for a moment, for I know not the value of my soul.
(John of the Cross, 'Prayer of the enamoured soul')

Ruth is the person who chooses God in choosing to
give herself to others. Hers is no sterile virginity; she is
immensely fruitful. Not merely does she bear a child,
but the whole community is enriched — especially her
beloved Naomi who turns from an embittered widow
into a joyful grandmother. And in the process Ruth
grows from dependence to being a woman in her own
right: love has indeed been stronger than death.

In Esther, conversely, we see no idyll of domestic bliss,
she is rather the victim of a royal 'marriage of
convenience'; yet she rivets our gaze as mistress of the
situation. Esther has no human love to sustain her in
accomplishing God's will; she is without warmth,
without interior joy, still she proceeds to do her duty.
What an example! Listen to her prayer:

As for ourselves, save us by your hand,
and come to my help, for I am alone
and have no one but you, Lord. . . .
Nor has your handmaid found pleasure
from the day of her promotion until now
except in you, Lord, God of Abraham.
O God whose strength prevails over all
listen to the voice of the desperate . . .
(cf. Esth. 4:17–19)

After this anguished plea Esther goes to petition the

71

King, outwardly composed and beautiful but inwardly frozen with fear. Her bravery is vindicated, and she then receives all she asks — and she asks not for her own sake but for the sake of her persecuted race. Her role is not personal but public.

Edith Stein loved the figure of Esther pleading for her people and saw in her an image of the consecrated woman who lives to intercede by her very being. She is one who prays to the Lord to accomplish what she is only too aware she cannot do alone by her unaided strength. Then she acts despite her natural repugnance. To *act* — that is the secret of spiritual growth; the king can refuse nothing to the one who comes before him in humble trust. 'What will you have, my Queen? What is your request?'

In the narratives of Ruth and Esther we see the close intermingling of circumstances and choice, love and duty, the one and the many: women whose paths *seem* very different, but whose fidelity to the demands of life involved each in a destiny beyond themselves.

'I wept because no one was found worthy', says the Book of Revelation. No one is 'worthy' to belong to the Lord as did these women who are symbols of the bride-soul and who bear their people upon their hearts. But from them we can learn something of what it means to be chosen by God to accomplish his plans, no matter what situation we find ourselves in. If we are 'determined to go with him' (Ruth 1:18) he will bring us to fulfilled womanhood in a way that is unique to each individual.

In Mary of Nazareth we see the prime example of the bride-soul as she moves from untouchability at the

Annunciation to availability in the Visitation. She moves from being an untainted, emotionally unexplored girl to the maturity of being mother and wife at the Nativity . . . and thence to the foot of the Cross. In her the whole gamut of life is lived with and for the Lord, and so she is 'his delight, his joy, his comfort, and most pleasing to him above all creation' (Julian, *Rev.* ch. 25).

Bearing His Likeness

The face is the most personal manifestation of individuality; it is the 'external heart'; as we are within so we become without.

A man's heart moulds his expression whether for better or worse.
(Ecclus. 13:25)

We might say that we are born with our features, but we make our own face. Often youthful beauty turns to hardness, while early plainness becomes full of character, born of wisdom and acceptance of life.

The wisdom of a man lends brightness to his face; his face, once grim, is altered. (Eccles. 8:1)

Those who live together over a long time can also come to look alike because they think alike, they reflect each other. Those who live with the Lord, think with the Lord, spend time in silence with the Lord, become his mirrors. His face is reflected in theirs in such a way that they become his living images, radiant with his glory (2 Cor. 3:18). And to bear the face of Christ is to show him to the world re-incarnate in human flesh, just as Jesus was the living image, the face of the Father, for men (2 Cor. 4:6). 'Philip, he who has seen me has seen the Father' (John 14:9).

Hieronymous Bosch painted a picture of the way of the Cross in which the face of Jesus has just been wiped by the legendary Veronica. She, in the midst of a crowd of hideous caricatures, gently carries the image of Christ on her precious cloth — her eyes and his both downcast in silent adoration.

Veronica is not a biblical woman, but a figure of Christian devotion. She symbolises *some*body doing *some*thing for a suffering fellow-being. She was not constrained to do it as was Simon of Cyrene, she was not simply bewailing another's fate as were the daughters of Jerusalem, nor was she deeply involved personally as was Mary in her maternal anguish. Veronica was just performing an act of kindness to another in defiance of public opinion, an act springing from a courageous heart, the human act of wiping the battered face of a suffering man. She was doing nothing specifically religious, and yet this woman received the imprint of Christ as a permanent gift — the *vera ikon*, 'true image' — of the One she had wanted to console. In Bosch's picture we see that the precious cloth of Christ's countenance covers her whole person, she bears the Lord for all to see. For wiping the face of an apparent criminal, degraded and shunned, she became the one blessed with knowing that beneath the outward appearance, beneath the sweat, blood and tears on the surface, lay the features of the most beautiful of the sons of men.

Here on earth we too see the face of Christ above all as a sorrowful face, marred by the sins of others; the way to the radiant vision of the Lord is by the way of the Cross. God shows his deepest love for us through the suffering servant, and in his Passion he demonstrates that love in a pre-eminent way.

For us to become like Jesus in glory means to accompany him in sorrow. His features will never be imprinted on our own unless, like St Thérèse, we learn to recognise and welcome him in things that, humanly speaking, seem unlovely: nearly always his face will have been disfigured and degraded by human hands — we can encounter him only in faith, faith that he abides in the poor, the needy, the despised.

O consider this, that your Divine Face
was unknown even to your brethren.
But you left us your image so still and bright
and, Lord, you know I recognised you.
Through the tear-stained veil
Face of the Eternal, I saw you radiant.
How your veiled countenance
comforts and delights my heart.
O consider this!
(St Thérèse, 'Remember Thou' v. 24)

If we are not alert as a Veronica, Christ will pass by us unnoticed and unrecognised.

We may wonder why the Veronica motif has become so popular when her existence has no basis in historical fact? Surely it is because here is something that we instinctively feel to be right. Veronica stands for those countless ordinary yet selfless acts of kindness done every day to Christ, and for Christ, in others.

In so many ways there is a reaching out beyond the boundaries of a religious or class-centred society. The human touch breaks in suddenly upon situations that would otherwise be totally inhuman. The cloth of Veronica shines out in contrast to the cloth with which Christ was blindfolded and mocked. The human touch

brings tears to the eyes of Eugenia Ginsberg when, in the wastes of a Siberian camp, a few women make toast to welcome her to her new 'home'. It is reflected in Mother Maria, the Orthodox highly unorthodox nun of Ravensbruck, who did what she could to give dignity to women deprived of all self-respect.

The charity of Veronica is no merely conventional act, like the giving of a draught of myrrh before crucifixion. It is a gesture of pure love arising in answer to the need of the moment; it is Mary of Bethany anointing the Lord, and Martha preparing sandwiches for the journey. No law can dictate the right response here; it isn't a question of in such and such a situation I do this, in another situation I do that. We have to be sensitive, intuitive to what to do or say in each specific case. And this will become more refined as we become more Christlike.

We can obviously connect the action of a Veronica with works of mercy: tending the Lord in the sick, the dying, the mentally ill, the prisoner, but there is another aspect too. Emotional wounds embitter the spirit, harden the outlook, or there are what seem insurmountable difficulties of temperament and character. We all have these in some degree, we all are bearers of the suffering face of Christ for others. As Julian put it:

> To bring his servants to bliss the Lord lays on each one he loves some particular thing, which, while it carries no blame in his sight, causes them to be blamed by the world, despised, scorned, mocked, rejected. This he does to forestall any hurt they might get from the pomps and vanities of this sinful world, to prepare their way to heaven, and to exalt them in his everlasting bliss. (*Rev.* ch. 28)

At times when we ourselves are weighed down under our 'particular thing' and are the suffering Christ for others, we can be gladdened by a gesture of kindness, someone reaching out to us; then we are made aware that we are loved even in our worst moments. 'A love that cannot, will not, be broken by sin is rocklike and quite astonishing', says Julian; we all need to give and receive this type of love and so be in contact with divine Love. We each need a Veronica in our lives to discover the beauty beneath the ugliness, the smoothness beneath the scars. Then there are moments when conversely *we* take the role of Veronica, often without knowing it. She had no idea *who* she had helped until later, had no idea there would be anything in it for her. It was only *afterwards* that she knew something wonderful had come to pass; there was imprinted on her veil the face of the Son of God in the act of redeeming us.

So, to be conformed to the likeness of Jesus upon earth, to bear his image, is a two-way process. It means reaching out to others in their pain and thus receiving the imprint of Christ through comforting him in his passion; and it means *being* him too — whether in our weakness or in our joy, so that through us others are brought into contact with the Lord.

Surely as time goes on therefore our own face should take on something of his compassion, his understanding, his wisdom. Then as Jesus could say, 'He who has seen me has seen the Father', so others can say of us, 'whoever sees her, sees Jesus'.

A New Song

How is happiness, sorrow, love expressed? By song. Hannah sings at the birth of Samuel, Miriam sings at the Red Sea, Jeremiah laments over Jerusalem and Mary bursts forth into her Magnificat. Even nature joins the symphony of praise.

> Let the wilderness and the dry-lands exult,
> let the wasteland rejoice and bloom,
> let it bring forth flowers like the jonquil,
> let it rejoice and sing for joy. (Isa. 35:1)

Music is a 'heavenly gift' for it speaks to us at a level deeper than words.

John of the Cross' *Spiritual Canticle* is filled with music as an expression of the soul's union with God. The soul on the fringes of contemplation, he says, is like the sparrow in that 'it sings unto God with sweetness' (st. xv) and union itself has all the freshness and soaring joy of the full-throated nightingale:

> As the song of the nightingale is heard in the spring of the year, when the cold and rain and changes of winter are past, filling the ear with melody and the mind with joy so in the true intercourse and transformation of love which takes place in this life, the

81

bride . . . becomes conscious of a new spring in which she hears the voice of the bridegroom who is her sweet nightingale, renewing and refreshing the very substance of her soul. (st. xxxix)

Music is indeed the language of lovers, and a hymn or song has the power to evoke a whole world of heightened awareness.

In its understanding of Mary, the liturgy puts before us the image of her life as a new song, just as it does in the blessing bestowed at Religious Profession. In fact *every* life is its own unique song, new because it has never been sung until enshrined in this particular life. The song of our own life has been breathed into us, 'inspired' by the Spirit of God himself.

Like Mary, then, we must give thanks, tell our God's greatness, rejoice in him with all we have and are. Thanksgiving is the basic attitude of a soul rooted in biblical spirituality. Our response to God's gift of his Son, and all the blessings that flow from this gift, can only be gratitude and wonder. 'It is God's will that I see myself as much bound to him in loving gratitude as if all he had ever done had been done for me alone. In his heart everyone should think this of his lover' (Julian, *Rev.* ch. 65). When we thank God, when we praise him, we make him present again in our lives. A heart full of song helps us to make God our centre, have him as our constant refrain, so that we live by faith in his love, seeing all creation in a new light.

My beloved is the mountains,
the solitary wooded valleys . . .
The tranquil night
at the approaches of dawn,

the silent music
the murmuring solitude.
    (John of the Cross, *Spiritual Canticle* st. xiv–xv)

Thanksgiving, as Julian points out, brings 'joy and gratitude within', and this is reflected in our actual bearing. The singer cannot be held bound by sadness but makes his way beyond it to rest in the beauty of the melody of God.

Joy is the seal of selflessness. How can we not be deeply happy if we know ourselves to be loved by the Lord? And by joy the love of God in us is made known to others. Jesus knew joy at Nazareth in the home of Mary and Joseph; to the larger world it seemed such a constricted, limited environment, but to him it contained all that was necessary for blessedness. And so can our poor, limited human lives contain the ingredients for God's music. We must let him then draw harmonies from our discords — thus we too can have a part in the great Magnificat symphony of eternity.